50 Japanese Rice and Sushi Dishes

By: Kelly Johnson

Table of Contents

- Sushi (Nigiri)
- Sashimi
- Temaki (Hand Roll)
- Maki Sushi
- Uramaki (Inside-out Roll)
- Chirashi Sushi
- Oshi Sushi (Pressed Sushi)
- Inari Sushi
- Gunkan Maki
- Ebi Sushi (Shrimp Sushi)
- Maguro Sushi (Tuna Sushi)
- Toro Sushi (Fatty Tuna Sushi)
- Ikura Sushi (Salmon Roe Sushi)
- Unagi Sushi (Grilled Eel Sushi)
- Tamago Sushi (Sweet Omelette Sushi)
- California Roll
- Dragon Roll
- Spicy Tuna Roll
- Rainbow Roll
- Boston Roll
- Tekka Maki (Tuna Roll)
- Kappa Maki (Cucumber Roll)
- Oshinko Maki (Pickled Radish Roll)
- Tori Teriyaki Sushi
- Futo Maki (Large Roll)
- Edomae Sushi
- Yaki Onigiri (Grilled Rice Ball)
- Onigiri (Rice Ball)
- Donburi (Rice Bowl)
- Gyudon (Beef Bowl)
- Katsudon (Pork Cutlet Bowl)
- Oyako Donburi (Chicken and Egg Bowl)
- Unadon (Grilled Eel Rice Bowl)
- Tamago Donburi (Egg Bowl)
- Zosui (Rice Soup)

- Takikomi Gohan (Seasoned Rice)
- Ikura Don (Salmon Roe Bowl)
- Chirashidon (Scattered Sushi Bowl)
- Kamameshi (Rice Cooked in a Pot)
- Gyoza Rice Bowl
- Tantanmen Rice
- Hainanese Chicken Rice
- Kurumi Gohan (Walnut Rice)
- Yaki Gohan (Fried Rice)
- Tofu Donburi (Tofu Rice Bowl)
- Miso Gohan (Miso Rice)
- Karaage Donburi (Fried Chicken Bowl)
- Bento (Japanese Lunch Box)
- Aburi Sushi (Seared Sushi)
- Nama Sashimi (Raw Fish Sashimi)

Nigiri Sushi

Ingredients:

- **Sushi rice** (about 1 ½ cups uncooked)
- **Water** (about 1 ¾ cups, for cooking rice)
- **Rice vinegar** (3 tbsp)
- **Sugar** (2 tbsp)
- **Salt** (1 tsp)
- **Fresh fish** (like tuna, salmon, or shrimp – sliced into thin pieces)
- **Wasabi** (optional)
- **Soy sauce** (for serving)

Equipment:

- Rice cooker or pot
- Wooden spoon or spatula
- Small bowl of water (to prevent sticking)
- Sharp knife

Instructions:

1. **Cook the Rice:**

    - Rinse the sushi rice in cold water until the water runs clear.
    - Cook the rice according to the rice cooker's instructions, or in a pot with 1 ¾ cups of water. After cooking, let it rest for about 10 minutes.

2. **Season the Rice:**

    - In a small saucepan, combine the rice vinegar, sugar, and salt. Heat over low until the sugar and salt dissolve completely (don't boil).
    - Once the rice has rested, transfer it to a large bowl and gently fold in the vinegar mixture. Let the rice cool to room temperature.

3. **Prepare the Fish:**

    - Slice your fish into thin, ¼-inch pieces. It's important that the fish is very fresh and of sushi grade.

4. **Shape the Rice:**

    - Wet your hands with water to prevent the rice from sticking.

    - Take a small amount of sushi rice (about a tablespoon), and mold it into an oblong mound using your fingers. You want it compact but not too tight.
5. **Assemble the Nigiri:**
    - Place a small amount of wasabi on top of the rice (optional).
    - Gently place a slice of fish on top of the rice mound, pressing it lightly to ensure it sticks.
6. **Serve:**
    - Arrange your Nigiri on a plate and serve with soy sauce for dipping.

Sashimi

Ingredients:

- Fresh fish (like tuna, salmon, or yellowtail) – sushi grade, sliced thinly
- Soy sauce
- Wasabi
- Pickled ginger (optional)

Instructions:

1. **Prepare the Fish:**
   - Slice the fish into thin pieces (about ¼ inch thick).
   - Make sure to use a sharp knife for clean cuts.
2. **Serve:**
   - Arrange the slices of fish on a plate.
   - Serve with soy sauce, wasabi, and pickled ginger on the side.

Enjoy your Sashimi!

Temaki (Hand Roll)

Ingredients:

- **Sushi rice** (prepared as per Nigiri recipe)
- **Nori (seaweed)** sheets
- **Fresh fish** (like tuna, salmon, or shrimp)
- **Vegetables** (like cucumber, avocado, or daikon radish)
- **Wasabi** (optional)
- **Soy sauce** (for dipping)

Instructions:

1. **Prepare the Fillings:**
   - Slice the fish and vegetables into thin strips.
2. **Assemble the Hand Roll:**
   - Place a sheet of nori on a flat surface.
   - Spread a small amount of sushi rice onto the nori (leaving one edge free).
   - Add your choice of fish and vegetables on top.
   - Roll the nori into a cone shape, folding it tightly to form the hand roll.
3. **Serve:**
   - Serve immediately with soy sauce and wasabi on the side.

Maki Sushi

Ingredients:

- **Sushi rice** (prepared as per Nigiri recipe)
- **Nori (seaweed)** sheets
- **Fresh fish** (like tuna, salmon, or shrimp)
- **Vegetables** (like cucumber, avocado, or pickled radish)
- **Soy sauce** (for dipping)
- **Bamboo sushi mat** (for rolling)

Instructions:

1. **Prepare the Fillings:**
    - Slice the fish and vegetables into long, thin strips.
2. **Assemble the Maki Roll:**
    - Lay a sheet of nori on a bamboo sushi mat.
    - Spread a thin layer of sushi rice on the nori, leaving a 1-inch border at the top.
    - Add fish and vegetables along the center of the rice.
3. **Roll the Maki:**
    - Using the bamboo mat, gently roll the nori from the bottom up, pressing lightly to form a cylinder.
    - Once rolled, slice the roll into bite-sized pieces.
4. **Serve:**
    - Serve with soy sauce, wasabi, and pickled ginger on the side.

Uramaki (Inside-out Roll)

Ingredients:

- **Sushi rice** (prepared as per Nigiri recipe)
- **Nori (seaweed)** sheets
- **Fresh fish** (like tuna, salmon, or shrimp)
- **Vegetables** (like cucumber, avocado, or pickled radish)
- **Sesame seeds** or **fish roe** (optional, for coating)
- **Soy sauce** (for dipping)
- **Bamboo sushi mat** (for rolling)

Instructions:

1. **Prepare the Fillings:**
   - Slice the fish and vegetables into thin strips.
2. **Prepare the Rice:**
   - Lightly wet your hands to prevent the rice from sticking.
3. **Assemble the Uramaki Roll:**
   - Lay a sheet of nori on a bamboo sushi mat, shiny side down.
   - Spread a thin layer of sushi rice evenly over the nori.
   - Sprinkle sesame seeds or fish roe over the rice (optional).
   - Flip the nori so the rice is on the bottom.
4. **Add the Fillings:**
   - Place fish and vegetables along the center of the nori.
5. **Roll the Uramaki:**
   - Carefully roll the sushi from the bottom up using the bamboo mat, pressing gently to form the roll.
6. **Serve:**
   - Slice the roll into bite-sized pieces and serve with soy sauce, wasabi, and pickled ginger on the side.

Chirashi Sushi

Ingredients:

- **Sushi rice** (prepared as per Nigiri recipe)
- **Fresh fish** (like tuna, salmon, shrimp, or yellowtail)
- **Vegetables** (like cucumber, avocado, and shredded daikon radish)
- **Pickled ginger**
- **Soy sauce** (for dipping)
- **Sesame seeds** (optional)

Instructions:

1. **Prepare the Fish and Vegetables:**
    - Slice the fish into thin pieces.
    - Cut the vegetables into small matchstick pieces or thin slices.
2. **Assemble the Chirashi:**
    - Place a bed of sushi rice in a large bowl.
    - Arrange the fish and vegetables on top of the rice, creating a colorful spread.
    - Garnish with sesame seeds and pickled ginger.
3. **Serve:**
    - Serve with soy sauce and wasabi on the side.

Oshi Sushi (Pressed Sushi)

Ingredients:

- **Sushi rice** (prepared as per Nigiri recipe)
- **Fresh fish** (like tuna or salmon)
- **Nori (seaweed)** sheets
- **Bamboo sushi mat** (for pressing)
- **Soy sauce** (for dipping)

Instructions:

1. **Prepare the Fish:**
    - Slice the fish into small, uniform pieces.
2. **Press the Sushi:**
    - Place a layer of sushi rice into a sushi box or a similar container.
    - Press the rice gently but firmly.
    - Place a layer of fish on top of the rice, pressing it down with the lid of the box or a flat surface.
3. **Slice and Serve:**
    - Once pressed, remove the lid and slice the block into small squares or rectangles.
    - Serve with soy sauce on the side.

Inari Sushi

Ingredients:

- **Sushi rice** (prepared as per Nigiri recipe)
- **Inari age (sweet fried tofu pockets)**
- **Soy sauce** (for dipping)

Instructions:

1. **Prepare the Sushi Rice:**
    - Prepare the sushi rice as usual.
2. **Assemble the Inari Sushi:**
    - Gently open the tofu pockets and fill them with sushi rice.
    - Gently press the rice inside the tofu pockets to pack it in.
3. **Serve:**
    - Serve with soy sauce on the side.

Gunkan Maki

Ingredients:

- **Sushi rice** (prepared as per Nigiri recipe)
- **Nori (seaweed)** sheets
- **Fresh fish or roe** (like tuna, salmon roe, or sea urchin)
- **Soy sauce** (for dipping)

Instructions:

1. **Prepare the Rice:**
    - Prepare sushi rice and let it cool to room temperature.
2. **Assemble the Gunkan Maki:**
    - Cut a strip of nori and wrap it around a small mound of sushi rice, forming a "boat."
    - Fill the center with your choice of fish, roe, or other toppings.
3. **Serve:**
    - Serve immediately with soy sauce.

Ebi Sushi (Shrimp Sushi)

Ingredients:

- **Sushi rice** (prepared as per Nigiri recipe)
- **Fresh shrimp** (boiled or grilled)
- **Nori (seaweed)** (optional for garnish)
- **Soy sauce** (for dipping)

Instructions:

1. **Prepare the Shrimp:**
   - Boil or grill the shrimp, removing the shells and tails.
2. **Assemble the Ebi Sushi:**
   - Mold the sushi rice into small oval shapes.
   - Place a piece of shrimp on top of each rice mound, pressing gently to secure.
3. **Serve:**
   - Serve with soy sauce and optional garnish of nori.

Maguro Sushi (Tuna Sushi)

Ingredients:

- **Sushi rice** (prepared as per Nigiri recipe)
- **Fresh tuna** (sliced thinly)
- **Soy sauce** (for dipping)

Instructions:

1. **Prepare the Tuna:**
    - Slice the fresh tuna into thin, bite-sized pieces.
2. **Assemble the Maguro Sushi:**
    - Mold the sushi rice into oval-shaped mounds.
    - Place a slice of tuna on top of the rice and press gently.
3. **Serve:**
    - Serve with soy sauce on the side.

Toro Sushi (Fatty Tuna Sushi)

Ingredients:

- **Sushi rice** (prepared as per Nigiri recipe)
- **Fatty tuna (Toro)** (sliced thinly)
- **Soy sauce** (for dipping)

Instructions:

1. **Prepare the Toro:**
    - Slice the fatty tuna (Toro) into thin, delicate pieces.
2. **Assemble the Toro Sushi:**
    - Mold the sushi rice into small oval shapes.
    - Place a slice of Toro on top of the rice and press gently.
3. **Serve:**
    - Serve with soy sauce.

Ikura Sushi (Salmon Roe Sushi)

Ingredients:

- **Sushi rice** (prepared as per Nigiri recipe)
- **Salmon roe (Ikura)**
- **Nori (seaweed)** (optional for garnish)
- **Soy sauce** (for dipping)

Instructions:

1. **Prepare the Sushi Rice:**
   - Prepare the sushi rice as usual.
2. **Assemble the Ikura Sushi:**
   - Mold the sushi rice into small oval shapes.
   - Place a spoonful of salmon roe (Ikura) on top of the rice.
3. **Serve:**
   - Serve with soy sauce on the side.

Unagi Sushi (Grilled Eel Sushi)

Ingredients:

- **Sushi rice** (prepared as per Nigiri recipe)
- **Grilled eel (Unagi)** (sliced)
- **Unagi sauce (sweet soy-based glaze)**
- **Soy sauce** (for dipping)

Instructions:

1. **Prepare the Eel:**
   - Grill the eel and brush with Unagi sauce.
   - Slice the grilled eel into thin pieces.
2. **Assemble the Unagi Sushi:**
   - Mold the sushi rice into small oval shapes.
   - Place a piece of grilled eel on top of the rice and press gently.
3. **Serve:**
   - Serve with soy sauce on the side.

Tamago Sushi (Sweet Omelette Sushi)

Ingredients:

- **Sushi rice** (prepared as per Nigiri recipe)
- **Eggs** (3-4)
- **Sugar** (1 tbsp)
- **Soy sauce** (1 tbsp)
- **Mirin** (1 tbsp)
- **Nori (seaweed)** (optional for garnish)

Instructions:

1. **Prepare the Tamago (Sweet Omelette):**
    - In a bowl, whisk eggs, sugar, soy sauce, and mirin together.
    - Heat a non-stick pan and lightly oil it. Pour a small amount of the egg mixture into the pan, swirling to coat evenly.
    - Cook each layer of egg, rolling it up as you go, until you've used all the egg mixture.
    - Slice the rolled omelette into small pieces.
2. **Assemble the Tamago Sushi:**
    - Mold the sushi rice into small oval shapes.
    - Place a piece of the tamago (sweet omelette) on top of the rice and press gently.
3. **Serve:**
    - Optionally, garnish with nori.

California Roll

Ingredients:

- **Sushi rice** (prepared as per Nigiri recipe)
- **Nori (seaweed)** sheets
- **Crab meat** (real or imitation)
- **Avocado** (sliced)
- **Cucumber** (sliced thinly)
- **Soy sauce** (for dipping)

Instructions:

1. **Prepare the Sushi Rice:**

    - Prepare sushi rice and set aside.
2. **Assemble the California Roll:**

    - Place a sheet of nori on a bamboo mat.
    - Spread an even layer of rice on the nori, leaving about 1 inch at the top.
    - Place crab meat, avocado, and cucumber along the bottom edge of the rice.
    - Roll tightly with the bamboo mat, using the exposed nori edge to seal the roll.
3. **Slice and Serve:**

    - Slice the roll into bite-sized pieces.
    - Serve with soy sauce.

Dragon Roll

Ingredients:

- **Sushi rice** (prepared as per Nigiri recipe)
- **Nori (seaweed)** sheets
- **Shrimp tempura** (or eel)
- **Avocado** (sliced)
- **Cucumber** (sliced thinly)
- **Eel sauce** (for drizzling)
- **Soy sauce** (for dipping)

Instructions:

1. **Prepare the Sushi Rice:**

    - Prepare sushi rice and set aside.

2. **Assemble the Dragon Roll:**

    - Place a sheet of nori on a bamboo mat.
    - Spread an even layer of rice on the nori.
    - Place shrimp tempura (or eel), avocado, and cucumber along the bottom edge of the rice.
    - Roll tightly with the bamboo mat.
    - Slice the roll into bite-sized pieces.

3. **Garnish and Serve:**

    - Top the roll with thin slices of avocado arranged like dragon scales.
    - Drizzle eel sauce over the roll.
    - Serve with soy sauce.

Spicy Tuna Roll

Ingredients:

- **Sushi rice** (prepared as per Nigiri recipe)
- **Nori (seaweed)** sheets
- **Fresh tuna** (finely diced)
- **Sriracha sauce** (or other spicy sauce)
- **Soy sauce** (for dipping)

Instructions:

1. **Prepare the Sushi Rice:**

   - Prepare sushi rice and set aside.

2. **Prepare the Spicy Tuna:**

   - Mix the diced tuna with sriracha sauce to your desired spice level.

3. **Assemble the Spicy Tuna Roll:**

   - Place a sheet of nori on a bamboo mat.
   - Spread an even layer of rice on the nori.
   - Add the spicy tuna mixture along the bottom edge of the rice.
   - Roll tightly with the bamboo mat.

4. **Slice and Serve:**

   - Slice the roll into bite-sized pieces.
   - Serve with soy sauce.

Rainbow Roll

Ingredients:

- **Sushi rice** (prepared as per Nigiri recipe)
- **Nori (seaweed)** sheets
- **California roll** (prepared from the California Roll recipe)
- **Sliced sashimi-grade fish** (like tuna, salmon, and avocado)
- **Soy sauce** (for dipping)

Instructions:

1. **Prepare the California Roll:**
   - Make a California roll using the ingredients and method from the California Roll recipe.
2. **Assemble the Rainbow Roll:**
   - Slice the California roll into bite-sized pieces.
   - Arrange slices of sashimi-grade fish (like tuna, salmon) and avocado on top of each piece of California roll.
3. **Serve:**
   - Serve with soy sauce.

Boston Roll

Ingredients:

- **Sushi rice** (prepared as per Nigiri recipe)
- **Nori (seaweed)** sheets
- **Cooked shrimp** (or lobster)
- **Avocado** (sliced)
- **Cucumber** (sliced thinly)
- **Lemon juice**
- **Soy sauce** (for dipping)

Instructions:

1. **Prepare the Sushi Rice:**

    - Prepare sushi rice and set aside.

2. **Assemble the Boston Roll:**

    - Place a sheet of nori on a bamboo mat.
    - Spread an even layer of rice on the nori.
    - Place shrimp (or lobster), avocado, and cucumber along the bottom edge of the rice.
    - Roll tightly with the bamboo mat.

3. **Serve:**

    - Slice the roll into bite-sized pieces.
    - Serve with soy sauce and a drizzle of lemon juice.

Tekka Maki (Tuna Roll)

Ingredients:

- **Sushi rice** (prepared as per Nigiri recipe)
- **Nori (seaweed)** sheets
- **Fresh tuna** (sliced into strips)
- **Soy sauce** (for dipping)

Instructions:

1. **Prepare the Sushi Rice:**

    - Prepare sushi rice and set aside.
2. **Assemble the Tekka Maki:**

    - Place a sheet of nori on a bamboo mat.
    - Spread an even layer of rice on the nori.
    - Place strips of fresh tuna along the bottom edge of the rice.
    - Roll tightly with the bamboo mat.
3. **Slice and Serve:**

    - Slice the roll into bite-sized pieces.
    - Serve with soy sauce.

Kappa Maki (Cucumber Roll)

Ingredients:

- **Sushi rice** (prepared as per Nigiri recipe)
- **Nori (seaweed)** sheets
- **Cucumber** (sliced into strips)
- **Soy sauce** (for dipping)

Instructions:

1. **Prepare the Sushi Rice:**

    - Prepare sushi rice and set aside.
2. **Assemble the Kappa Maki:**

    - Place a sheet of nori on a bamboo mat.
    - Spread an even layer of rice on the nori.
    - Place cucumber strips along the bottom edge of the rice.
    - Roll tightly with the bamboo mat.
3. **Slice and Serve:**

    - Slice the roll into bite-sized pieces.
    - Serve with soy sauce.

Oshinko Maki (Pickled Radish Roll)

Ingredients:

- **Sushi rice** (prepared as per Nigiri recipe)
- **Nori (seaweed)** sheets
- **Pickled radish (Oshinko)** (sliced into strips)
- **Soy sauce** (for dipping)

Instructions:

1. **Prepare the Sushi Rice:**

    - Prepare sushi rice and set aside.
2. **Assemble the Oshinko Maki:**

    - Place a sheet of nori on a bamboo mat.
    - Spread an even layer of rice on the nori.
    - Place pickled radish strips along the bottom edge of the rice.
    - Roll tightly with the bamboo mat.
3. **Slice and Serve:**

    - Slice the roll into bite-sized pieces.
    - Serve with soy sauce.

Tori Teriyaki Sushi

Ingredients:

- **Sushi rice** (prepared as per Nigiri recipe)
- **Cooked chicken (Tori Teriyaki)** (sliced)
- **Soy sauce** (for dipping)

Instructions:

1. **Prepare the Sushi Rice:**

    - Prepare sushi rice and set aside.
2. **Prepare the Chicken:**

    - Cook chicken in teriyaki sauce until tender and slice thinly.
3. **Assemble the Tori Teriyaki Sushi:**

    - Mold the sushi rice into small oval shapes.
    - Place a slice of teriyaki chicken on top of the rice and press gently.
4. **Serve:**

    - Serve with soy sauce.

Futo Maki (Large Roll)

Ingredients:

- **Sushi rice** (prepared as per Nigiri recipe)
- **Nori (seaweed)** sheets
- **Variety of fillings** (such as avocado, cucumber, egg, fish, or pickled radish)
- **Soy sauce** (for dipping)

Instructions:

1. **Prepare the Sushi Rice:**

   - Prepare sushi rice and set aside.

2. **Assemble the Futo Maki:**

   - Place a sheet of nori on a bamboo mat.
   - Spread an even layer of rice on the nori, leaving a 1-inch border at the top.
   - Add a variety of fillings along the bottom edge of the rice.
   - Roll tightly with the bamboo mat.

3. **Slice and Serve:**

   - Slice the roll into thick pieces (larger than typical rolls).
   - Serve with soy sauce.

Edomae Sushi

Ingredients:

- **Sushi rice** (prepared as per Nigiri recipe)
- **Fresh fish** (like tuna, salmon, or yellowtail)
- **Soy sauce** (for dipping)
- **Wasabi** (optional)

Instructions:

1. **Prepare the Sushi Rice:**

    - Prepare sushi rice and set aside.

2. **Prepare the Fish:**

    - Slice the fish into thin pieces suitable for Edomae-style sushi (often served with a small dab of wasabi underneath).

3. **Assemble the Edomae Sushi:**

    - Mold the sushi rice into small oval shapes.
    - Place a slice of fish on top of each rice mound and press gently.

4. **Serve:**

    - Serve with soy sauce and wasabi on the side.

Yaki Onigiri (Grilled Rice Ball)

Ingredients:

- **Cooked sushi rice** (prepared as per Nigiri recipe)
- **Soy sauce** (for brushing)
- **Nori (seaweed)** (optional)
- **Sesame seeds** (optional)

Instructions:

1. **Form the Onigiri:**
    - Wet your hands and shape the rice into small triangular or oval rice balls.
2. **Grill the Rice Balls:**
    - Heat a grill or pan over medium heat.
    - Brush each rice ball lightly with soy sauce and grill until crispy on all sides.
3. **Serve:**
    - Optionally, garnish with nori or sesame seeds before serving.

Onigiri (Rice Ball)

Ingredients:

- **Cooked sushi rice** (prepared as per Nigiri recipe)
- **Filling** (like pickled plum, tuna, or salmon flakes)
- **Nori (seaweed)** sheets (optional)

Instructions:

1. **Form the Onigiri:**
    - Wet your hands and shape the rice into small triangular or oval rice balls.
    - If desired, add a small amount of your chosen filling in the center before forming the ball.
2. **Serve:**
    - Optionally, wrap the onigiri in a strip of nori before serving.

Donburi (Rice Bowl)

Ingredients:

- **Cooked rice**
- **Toppings** (like vegetables, meat, or seafood)
- **Soy sauce** or **teriyaki sauce** (optional)

Instructions:

1. **Prepare the Rice:**
    - Cook rice and place it into a large bowl.
2. **Add the Toppings:**
    - Add your choice of cooked vegetables, meat (like beef, chicken, or pork), or seafood on top of the rice.
3. **Serve:**
    - Optionally drizzle with soy sauce or teriyaki sauce before serving.

Gyudon (Beef Bowl)

Ingredients:

- **Cooked rice**
- **Thinly sliced beef** (like sirloin)
- **Onions** (sliced)
- **Soy sauce**
- **Mirin**
- **Sugar**
- **Dashi stock**
- **Pickled ginger** (optional)

Instructions:

1. **Prepare the Beef and Sauce:**

    - In a pan, heat dashi stock, soy sauce, mirin, and sugar. Bring to a simmer.
    - Add the sliced onions and cook until softened.
    - Add the beef and cook until tender.

2. **Assemble the Gyudon:**

    - Place a portion of rice in a bowl.
    - Spoon the beef and onion mixture over the rice.

3. **Serve:**

    - Optionally, top with pickled ginger and serve hot.

Katsudon (Pork Cutlet Bowl)

Ingredients:

- **Cooked rice**
- **Pork cutlet** (tonkatsu, breaded and fried)
- **Eggs** (beaten)
- **Onions** (sliced)
- **Soy sauce**
- **Mirin**
- **Dashi stock**

Instructions:

1. **Prepare the Tonkatsu (Pork Cutlet):**

    - Bread and fry a pork cutlet until golden and crispy. Slice into strips.

2. **Prepare the Sauce:**

    - In a pan, heat dashi stock, soy sauce, and mirin.
    - Add sliced onions and cook until softened.
    - Pour in the beaten eggs and let them cook slightly until they form a soft, cooked topping.

3. **Assemble the Katsudon:**

    - Place a portion of rice in a bowl.
    - Top with the sliced pork cutlet and egg mixture.

4. **Serve:**

    - Serve immediately while hot.

Oyako Donburi (Chicken and Egg Bowl)

Ingredients:

- **Cooked rice**
- **Chicken** (boneless, skinless)
- **Eggs** (beaten)
- **Onions** (sliced)
- **Soy sauce**
- **Mirin**
- **Dashi stock**

Instructions:

1. **Prepare the Chicken and Sauce:**

    - Slice chicken into bite-sized pieces and cook in a pan.
    - Add sliced onions and cook until tender.
    - Mix soy sauce, mirin, and dashi stock in the pan and bring to a simmer.

2. **Add the Eggs:**

    - Pour in the beaten eggs and let them cook until softly set.

3. **Assemble the Oyako Donburi:**

    - Place a portion of rice in a bowl.
    - Top with the chicken and egg mixture.

4. **Serve:**

    - Serve hot.

Unadon (Grilled Eel Rice Bowl)

Ingredients:

- **Cooked rice**
- **Grilled eel (Unagi)**
- **Unagi sauce** (sweet soy-based glaze)

Instructions:

1. **Prepare the Rice:**

    - Cook rice and place it in a large bowl.
2. **Prepare the Eel:**

    - Grill eel and brush with unagi sauce to coat.
3. **Assemble the Unadon:**

    - Place a portion of rice in a bowl.
    - Top with grilled eel and drizzle with more unagi sauce.
4. **Serve:**

    - Serve hot.

Tamago Donburi (Egg Bowl)

Ingredients:

- **Cooked rice**
- **Eggs** (beaten)
- **Soy sauce**
- **Mirin**

Instructions:

1. **Prepare the Eggs:**

    - In a pan, scramble the eggs with a little soy sauce and mirin until soft and fluffy.

2. **Assemble the Tamago Donburi:**

    - Place a portion of rice in a bowl.
    - Top with the scrambled eggs.

3. **Serve:**

    - Serve immediately while hot.

Zosui (Rice Soup)

Ingredients:

- **Cooked rice**
- **Dashi stock**
- **Chicken** (or pork, optional)
- **Mushrooms** (shiitake or enoki)
- **Ginger** (thinly sliced)
- **Soy sauce**
- **Egg** (optional, beaten)
- **Spring onions** (for garnish)

Instructions:

1. **Prepare the Soup:**

   - In a pot, bring dashi stock to a simmer.
   - Add sliced chicken or pork, mushrooms, and ginger.
   - Cook until the meat is tender.

2. **Add the Rice:**

   - Add the cooked rice to the pot and stir.

3. **Finish and Serve:**

   - Optionally, pour in a beaten egg and let it cook in the soup.
   - Garnish with spring onions before serving.

Takikomi Gohan (Seasoned Rice)

Ingredients:

- **Cooked rice**
- **Soy sauce**
- **Mirin**
- **Dashi stock**
- **Shiitake mushrooms** (or other mushrooms)
- **Carrot** (thinly sliced)
- **Chicken or other protein (optional)**

Instructions:

1. **Prepare the Seasoning:**

    - In a small pot, combine soy sauce, mirin, and dashi stock. Bring to a simmer.

2. **Prepare the Rice:**

    - Add the seasoning mix to the rice in a rice cooker or pot.
    - Add thinly sliced mushrooms, carrots, and optional chicken or other protein.

3. **Cook the Rice:**

    - Cook the rice as usual in a rice cooker or on the stove, absorbing all the seasoning flavors.

4. **Serve:**

    - Serve the seasoned rice in bowls.

Ikura Don (Salmon Roe Bowl)

Ingredients:

- **Cooked rice**
- **Salmon roe (Ikura)**
- **Soy sauce** (for drizzling)
- **Nori (seaweed)** (optional)

Instructions:

1. **Prepare the Rice:**

    - Cook the rice and place it in a bowl.
2. **Assemble the Bowl:**

    - Top the rice with a generous portion of salmon roe (Ikura).
3. **Serve:**

    - Optionally drizzle with soy sauce and garnish with nori strips before serving.

Chirashidon (Scattered Sushi Bowl)

Ingredients:

- **Sushi rice** (prepared as per Nigiri recipe)
- **Fresh sashimi-grade fish** (like tuna, salmon, or yellowtail)
- **Pickled ginger**
- **Cucumber** (sliced)
- **Avocado** (sliced)
- **Soy sauce** (for dipping)

Instructions:

1. **Prepare the Sushi Rice:**

    - Prepare sushi rice and place it in a large bowl.
2. **Assemble the Chirashidon:**

    - Scatter slices of fresh fish, cucumber, avocado, and pickled ginger on top of the sushi rice.
3. **Serve:**

    - Serve with soy sauce for dipping.

Kamameshi (Rice Cooked in a Pot)

Ingredients:

- **Cooked rice**
- **Dashi stock**
- **Chicken or pork (optional)**
- **Mushrooms**
- **Soy sauce**
- **Carrot** (sliced)

Instructions:

1. **Prepare the Ingredients:**

    - In a pot, layer your cooked rice with dashi stock, soy sauce, and optional protein (like chicken or pork).
    - Add sliced mushrooms and carrot.
2. **Cook the Rice:**

    - Cover and cook on low heat until the rice absorbs all the liquid and becomes tender.
3. **Serve:**

    - Serve hot from the pot.

Gyoza Rice Bowl

Ingredients:

- **Cooked rice**
- **Gyoza (dumplings)** (either homemade or store-bought)
- **Soy sauce** (for dipping)
- **Spring onions** (for garnish)

Instructions:

1. **Cook the Gyoza:**

    - Cook gyoza according to package instructions, typically by pan-frying and then steaming.

2. **Assemble the Bowl:**

    - Place a portion of cooked rice in a bowl.
    - Top with gyoza.

3. **Serve:**

    - Serve with soy sauce and garnish with spring onions.

Tantanmen Rice

Ingredients:

- **Cooked rice**
- **Ground pork**
- **Tantanmen sauce** (made with sesame paste, chili oil, and soy sauce)
- **Spring onions** (for garnish)
- **Peanuts** (crushed, for topping)

Instructions:

1. **Prepare the Tantanmen Sauce:**
    - Combine sesame paste, chili oil, soy sauce, and a little sugar to create the sauce.
2. **Cook the Pork:**
    - In a pan, cook ground pork until browned.
3. **Assemble the Rice:**
    - Place a portion of cooked rice in a bowl.
    - Top with the cooked pork and drizzle with tantanmen sauce.
4. **Serve:**
    - Garnish with crushed peanuts and spring onions.

Hainanese Chicken Rice

Ingredients:

- **Cooked rice**
- **Chicken** (boiled or steamed)
- **Chicken broth** (for cooking rice)
- **Cucumber** (sliced)
- **Soy sauce** (for dipping)

Instructions:

1. **Cook the Rice:**

    - Cook rice using chicken broth for added flavor.
2. **Prepare the Chicken:**

    - Boil or steam the chicken until fully cooked.
    - Slice the chicken into pieces.
3. **Assemble the Dish:**

    - Place a portion of rice in a bowl.
    - Top with sliced chicken and garnish with cucumber slices.
4. **Serve:**

    - Serve with soy sauce for dipping.

Kurumi Gohan (Walnut Rice)

Ingredients:

- **Cooked rice**
- **Walnuts** (toasted)
- **Soy sauce**
- **Mirin**

Instructions:

1. **Prepare the Walnuts:**

    - Toast walnuts in a dry pan until fragrant.
2. **Cook the Rice:**

    - Prepare the rice as usual and drizzle with soy sauce and mirin.
3. **Assemble the Rice:**

    - Stir toasted walnuts into the rice.
4. **Serve:**

    - Serve immediately.

Yaki Gohan (Fried Rice)

Ingredients:

- **Cooked rice** (preferably day-old)
- **Egg** (beaten)
- **Vegetables** (like peas, carrots, onions)
- **Soy sauce**
- **Sesame oil**
- **Green onions** (for garnish)

Instructions:

1. **Prepare the Fried Rice:**

    - Heat sesame oil in a pan and scramble the beaten egg.
    - Add the vegetables and stir-fry until tender.
    - Add the cooked rice and soy sauce. Stir to combine.

2. **Serve:**

    - Garnish with green onions before serving.

Tofu Donburi (Tofu Rice Bowl)

Ingredients:

- **Cooked rice**
- **Firm tofu** (pressed and cubed)
- **Soy sauce**
- **Mirin**
- **Green onions** (for garnish)
- **Sesame seeds** (optional)

Instructions:

1. **Prepare the Tofu:**

    - Press and cube the tofu. Cook in a pan until lightly browned.

2. **Prepare the Sauce:**

    - In the same pan, add soy sauce and mirin to create a light sauce.

3. **Assemble the Tofu Donburi:**

    - Place a portion of cooked rice in a bowl.
    - Top with the cooked tofu and sauce.

4. **Serve:**

    - Garnish with green onions and sesame seeds if desired.

Miso Gohan (Miso Rice)

Ingredients:

- **Cooked rice**
- **Miso paste** (white or red)
- **Dashi stock** (optional)
- **Green onions** (chopped, for garnish)
- **Sesame seeds** (optional)

Instructions:

1. **Prepare the Miso Sauce:**

    - In a small bowl, mix a spoonful of miso paste with a little dashi stock or water to make a smooth paste.

2. **Cook the Rice:**

    - Prepare the rice as usual.

3. **Combine:**

    - After cooking the rice, stir in the miso paste mixture until evenly distributed.

4. **Serve:**

    - Garnish with chopped green onions and sesame seeds before serving.

Karaage Donburi (Fried Chicken Bowl)

Ingredients:

- **Cooked rice**
- **Boneless chicken thighs** (cut into bite-sized pieces)
- **Cornstarch** (for coating)
- **Soy sauce**
- **Ginger** (grated)
- **Garlic** (minced)
- **Sesame oil** (for frying)
- **Spring onions** (chopped, for garnish)
- **Sesame seeds** (optional)

Instructions:

1. **Prepare the Marinade:**

    - In a bowl, mix soy sauce, grated ginger, minced garlic, and a bit of sesame oil. Marinate the chicken for 15-30 minutes.

2. **Coat the Chicken:**

    - Coat the marinated chicken pieces in cornstarch.

3. **Fry the Chicken:**

    - Heat sesame oil in a frying pan and fry the chicken until golden and crispy.

4. **Assemble the Bowl:**

    - Place a portion of cooked rice in a bowl and top with the crispy fried chicken.

5. **Serve:**

    - Garnish with spring onions and sesame seeds before serving.

Bento (Japanese Lunch Box)

Ingredients:

- **Cooked rice** (for the base)
- **Protein** (like teriyaki chicken, salmon, or beef)
- **Vegetables** (pickled, steamed, or stir-fried)
- **Egg** (boiled or tamagoyaki, Japanese omelette)
- **Pickles** (optional, like pickled radish)
- **Fruit** (optional, like orange slices or grapes)

Instructions:

1. **Prepare the Rice:**

    - Cook rice and let it cool slightly before packing it into the bento box.
2. **Prepare the Protein:**

    - Cook your choice of protein (teriyaki chicken, grilled salmon, etc.).
3. **Prepare the Sides:**

    - Cook or prepare vegetables (like stir-fried broccoli, pickled carrots, or steamed spinach).
    - Make tamagoyaki or boil an egg for the bento box.
4. **Assemble the Bento:**

    - Pack the rice, protein, vegetables, egg, and any sides or fruit into a compartmented bento box.
5. **Serve:**

    - Pack the bento for lunch or serve immediately.

Aburi Sushi (Seared Sushi)

Ingredients:

- **Sushi rice** (prepared as per Nigiri recipe)
- **Fresh fish** (like tuna, salmon, or scallops)
- **Soy sauce** (for dipping)
- **Wasabi** (optional)
- **Torch or grill** (for searing)

Instructions:

1. **Prepare the Sushi Rice:**

    - Prepare sushi rice and mold it into small oval-shaped portions.

2. **Prepare the Fish:**

    - Slice the fish into thin pieces suitable for sushi.

3. **Sear the Fish:**

    - Use a torch or grill to lightly sear the top of each fish slice for a few seconds until just caramelized.

4. **Assemble the Aburi Sushi:**

    - Place the seared fish slice on top of the molded sushi rice.

5. **Serve:**

    - Serve with soy sauce and wasabi on the side.

Nama Sashimi (Raw Fish Sashimi)

Ingredients:

- **Fresh sashimi-grade fish** (like tuna, salmon, or yellowtail)
- **Soy sauce** (for dipping)
- **Wasabi** (optional)
- **Ginger** (pickled)

Instructions:

1. **Prepare the Fish:**

    - Slice the sashimi-grade fish into thin, bite-sized pieces.
2. **Serve:**

    - Arrange the sashimi slices on a plate.
3. **Accompaniments:**

    - Serve with soy sauce, wasabi, and pickled ginger on the side for dipping.